THE SEA

Exploring Life on an Ocean Planet

Endpaper Photographs:
Philip Plisson

Design Coordinator, English-language edition: Sonia Chaghatzbanian

Library of Congress Cataloging-in-Publication Data

Plisson, Philip.
[Mer racontée aux enfants. English]
The Sea: Exploring Life on an Ocean Planet/Philip Plisson; text by Yvon Mauffret;
drawings by Emmanuel Cerisier; adapted by Robert Burleigh.
p. cm.
Summary: Text and photographs of storms, ports, pollution, diving, rescues, surfing, lighthouses, tides,
and many kinds of boats, plants, and animals reveal the world's oceans and the people who live on or near them.
ISBN 0-8109-4591-6
1. Ocean—Juvenile literature. 2. Ships—Juvenile literature. [1.
Ocean. 2. Ships.] I. Mauffret, Yvon. II. Cerisier, Emmanuel, ill. III.
Burleigh, Robert. IV. Title.

GC21.5.P5813 2003
551.46—dc21
2003000972

Printed and bound in Belgium
10 9 8 7 6 5 4 3 2 1

Harry N. Abrams, Inc.
100 Fifth Avenue
New York, N.Y. 10011
www.abramsbooks.com

Abrams is a subsidiary of
LA MARTINIÈRE
GROUPE

THE SEA
Exploring Life on an Ocean Planet

photographs by
PHILIP PLISSON

Adapted by
Robert Burleigh

Text by
Yvon Mauffret

Drawings by
Emmanuel Cerisier

HARRY N. ABRAMS, INC., PUBLISHERS

Contents

"My name is Marin, and my little cousin is Malo...

My grandfather's name is Philip, and when I see his eyes peering over the glasses he always lets slide down his nose so he can see me better, well, in those eyes I see the ocean.

It's an ocean that stretches on and on. My grandpa loves the sea like nobody else. He'd probably say he fell into the ocean when he was little. It's true.

Besides, when he was my age, he already had a camera. He would go in his flat-bottomed boat to photograph the boats in the channel. Before he went to sleep, he would develop his prints himself. I'm absolutely sure he didn't do his schoolwork during all that time.

When he got big, at eighteen, he left on a ship belonging to the French Navy, or the Royale, as we call it in France. It's a name that makes me dream. He was a seaman with a red pom-pom, and he sailed on a trip around the world. He saw all of the oceans. He did all of the small chores onboard. He made a little money, and that's how he could buy the camera of his dreams when he made a port of call in the Indian Ocean.

A fairy tale couldn't be any better: In 1991, he was named Painter of the Navy by the French Ministry of Defense, an unbelievable honor for his work as a seaman photographer. And, after being a sailor, he was promoted to officer!

You shouldn't laugh, my grandpa is darned proud of it. Especially when you consider that it was Cardinal Richelieu himself who thought up the idea of Official Navy Painters. That's right, the Richelieu whom you read about in history books about France, the minister under Louis XIII. Of course, at that time

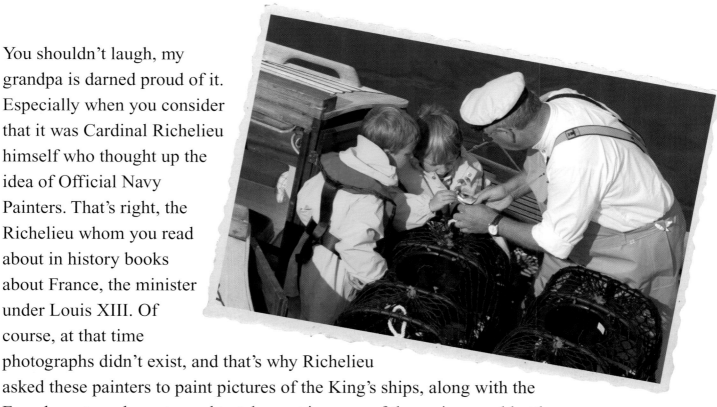

photographs didn't exist, and that's why Richelieu asked these painters to paint pictures of the King's ships, along with the French ports and coasts, and to take part in some of the major naval battles so that they could be captured on canvas.

Malo and I are very proud when grandpa wears his naval officer's uniform and his decorations at special events. And when, each time he signs a picture, he draws a navy anchor after his name, it's not to pretty things up, but it's because that means he is a real "Navy Painter." Besides, if you go to the Navy Museum in Paris, you'll see that I'm not just talking to hear myself talk. There are a lot of pictures with an anchor after the painter's signature.

Our grandpa has traveled a lot to take photos of boats all over the world. At the beginning, he photographed racing boats and the latest in beautiful yachts. But now, he would rather take pictures of Brittany and lighthouses to show everyone how beautiful the French coasts are. When he's with us in La Trinité, he tells Malo and me how to take beautiful pictures. First of all, you have to know what you're photographing. Then, you have to wait for hours to make sure the light is as beautiful as it can be. Very often, he photographs early in the morning or a few minutes before sunset.

On his beautiful red launch, the *Picture Fisherman*, he takes pictures of the coast and of working boats.

He also likes storms. When the sea becomes foam-white, he gets in the helicopter and the photos come out with an extra beauty, especially when the wind really howls and the waves are rough!

When we go to sea with him, we can easily see that the men who gain their living from the sea, the fishermen and oyster farmers, for example, are proud that he is photographing them. With him along, the boats and the sailors always look natural.

On grandpa's boats we learn to take pictures, but also how to sail. Grandpa's a super instructor, and a true sailor.

"I don't know if I'll be a photographer later on, like him, but I know already that I love the sea a lot. Malo does, too, and that's because of our grandpa."

The art of fishing on foot

The most popular activity on some coasts is probably fishing on foot. People fish this way when the tide reaveals a hidden universe of sea creatures.

No, the people in the photograph aren't just wading in high boots. They're fishing. During spring, when the tide goes out and the water recedes, an army of men, women, and children head to the sea. They are equipped with various tools: nets, scrapers, buckets, and bags. It's time to fish — on foot!

The sea is low and offers its treasures to anyone who wants to take them. There are prawns in the seagrass beds, crabs under stones, sole and dab hidden in the sand, mussels clinging to rocks, and clams buried several inches deep in the sand.

This invasion lasts for several hours. Then the sea rises again, chasing away before it all the people who came to the shore.

It's a guiltless pleasure, provided that the people fishing obey two simple rules: put back the stones that have been turned over, so that the animals that took refuge under them can still live there; and don't take small animals, but rather let them grow big so they can reproduce. If those who fish on foot follow these rules, they can happily come back again – and again.

cockle

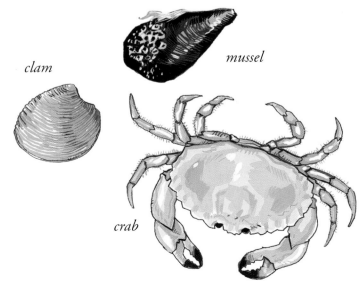

clam

mussel

crab

Boats leaving the port

Every four years, a great gathering of boats from throughout the world takes place at the port of Brest and at Port-Rhu in Douarnenez, France. Thousands of boats take part.

Trains have train stations, and ships have ports. It's there that ships unload their fish and other cargo, take on passengers, or are repaired when necessary.

Some ports, like those of New York and Los Angeles, are immense. Others are so small that only a single craft can manage to fit in. Yet they all serve the same purpose: to offer shelter to the boats that come in from the open sea.

Life in a big port never stops. The signal comes in that a large ship is arriving. Tugboats wait for it and guide it in to the wharf. After it docks, its holds are thrown open and huge cranes start to load or unload cargo. Dockworkers then make the cargo ready for shipping under the watchful eyes of customs officials. Supply boats provide the ship with whatever it needs. But after only a few hours, it's time to head out to sea once more. The ship is ready to continue its passage, while another waits to take its place along the wharf.

Fishermen caught in the currents

In the Raz de Sein, off the coast of France, bass fishermen risk their lives among the breakers to capture the king of fish.

The sea is so vast and the ship is so tiny. Can you see it among the whitecaps?

Early navigators who crossed the Atlantic wondered why their ships traveled faster when going from America to Europe than the other way around. Geographers who studied this problem discovered an ocean current they called the Gulf Stream. A current is a kind of river that travels through the ocean, triggered by the winds blowing over the surface.

The Gulf Stream begins in the warm waters of the Gulf of Mexico, heads north, and reaches the coasts of Europe, which it follows before plunging into the icy waters of the Arctic. It moves at a speed of about two and a half miles per hour. Ships that sail along the same route take advantage of this current.

Many other major ocean currents furrow the seas. Depending on the conditions of the seas where they are born, they bring cooler or warmer weather to areas off the coasts that they move along.

The *Norway,* flagship of the Norwegian fleet

The *France* was launched in 1954. Because it was excessively big and overly luxurious, France wasn't able to keep it. For twenty-five years, it has been the flagship of Norway's fleet and has been renamed the *Norway*.

The history of ocean liners, the ships that carry passengers, started early in the nineteenth century with the growing number of immigrants to the United States. But that was only the beginning. The golden age of ocean liners was between the two World Wars (1918-1939). Gigantic ships appeared that were true floating palaces. These ships (just look at the photograph!) could accommodate both multimillionaires and penniless immigrants.

At that time, the great seagoing nations (France, the United States, Great Britain, Norway, and Germany) competed over who could build the fastest, most luxurious ocean liner. Many beautiful ships were built. Every year, thousands of people sailed in this kind of ship over all of the world's oceans.

But times change. The airplane made its entrance. Air crossings became shorter and shorter, and less expensive. At last the liners had to give up the fight. All that's left for them today is the cruise, a voyage offered to tourists in love with the open sea and exotic landscapes.

Dolphin running before the stern of a ship

This ship seems to enjoy nosing forward just behind a playful dolphin.

It lives in the sea, and it has fins—but it isn't a fish. So what is it? It's a dolphin, a marine mammal belonging to the family of cetaceans, which includes other sea-dwellers such as the blue whale, the sperm whale, and the killer whale.

Dolphins possess many humanlike characteristics. The female dolphin gives birth after a gestation period of twelve months. She even breast-feeds her babies. Dolphins are social animals, too. They love to play, and often form groups of about one hundred.

Dolphins communicate with each other using a whole range of sounds, whistles, squeals, and squeaks. Scientists are attempting to decode this mysterious language, but they haven't yet been successful.

The species is being preserved for now, but there could be trouble ahead. The huge nets that fishermen spread out in certain parts of the oceans sometimes become deadly traps for dolphins. Each year, thousands of them are caught in these nets and suffocate to death.

Salmon farming

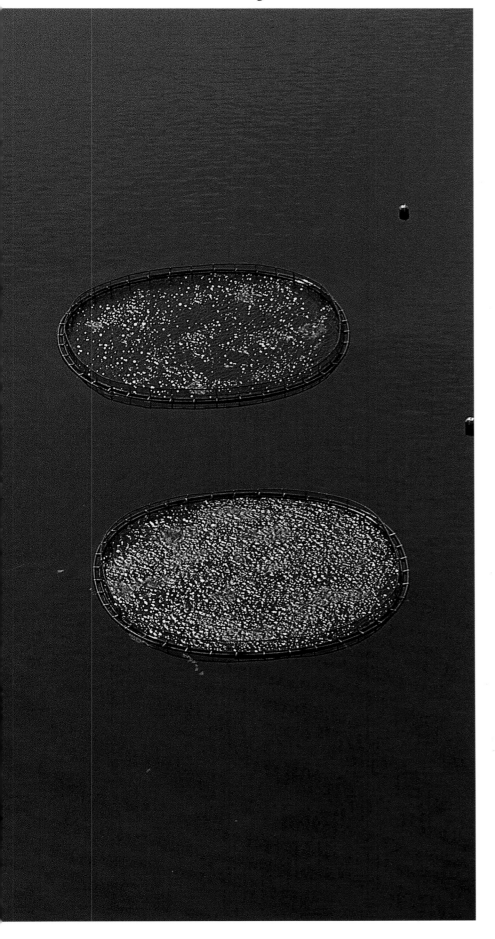

In Western Scotland, the deep lochs provide refuges that are especially well suited to fish farming.

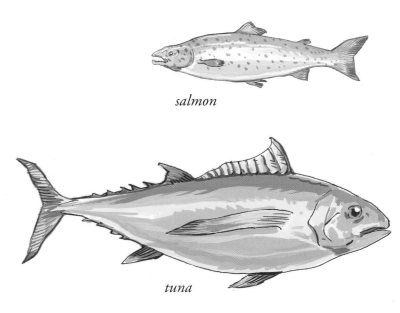

Can people "farm" fish, just as they grow corn and wheat? They can, and they do. Listen to this.

Raising fish, feeding them, caring for them, and selling them when they can be eaten — this process is called fish farming. For centuries, humans have counted exclusively on fishing to obtain fish. But as the world's expanding population has needed more food, scientists have developed fish farming to meet the demand.

Today we can cause fish eggs to hatch and baby fish to grow in captivity by providing the proper diet and good light and heat conditions. After three years, a bass egg turns into a beautiful fish weighing more than one-half a pound (even though it does not taste exactly like a wild fish). Bream, turbot, and sole are other fish that adapt well to the conditions required for fish farming.

Throughout the word, fish farming is progressing at a giant's pace. There are huge salmon farms in Norway and Canada, shrimp in Bangladesh, and the end is not yet in sight.

salmon

tuna

Surfer on a Polynesian beach

A surfer emerges from the foam after a punishing test with the sea.

It's difficult, it's dangerous, and it's breathtaking fun. And it goes on all over the world, wherever the great breakers rise out of the ocean and sweep toward shore. It's surfing.

The word *surf* refers to the backwash of the water, the powerful return of waves on themselves as they hit the shore. Those who surf ride these waves — all while balancing on a board.

For several decades, surfers have taken part in what is now much more than a sport — call it a lifestyle. They congregate in special places, or spots, all over the globe where the waves can be huge. To find a good spot, they will travel anywhere in the world, to Taapuna in Tahiti, to Tavarua in the Fiji Islands, as well as the California coast. Wherever the sea breaks, surfers are at home.

But take care. Many of these places are dangerous and are reserved for only the best surfers.

The helicopter carrier *Joan of Arc*

An Alouette III aircraft has just left the bridge of a navy helicopter carrier for a reconnaissance mission on the open sea off Argentina.

Every large country has built up a strong navy fleet to protect its shores. *Fleet* is a word used for a group of warships. This helicopter carrier is on a training mission in the ocean near South America.

The navy is the branch of the military that defends a country on the world's oceans.

Every large country's fleet must remain strong, relying on nuclear submarines and aircraft carriers, such as the one you see in the picture. Destroyers are used to escort these submarines and aircraft carriers. Minelayers position mines in the ocean, while minesweepers scoop them up. Tankers resupply the ships. There are other kinds of naval ships as well.

The ship you see in the picture is also a schooling ship where young officer graduates are trained. During a six-month run that takes them around the globe, the new officers learn in-depth their job as sailors.

Sailing for pleasure

Yachting refers to the pleasure of navigating by sail or motor. In the calm of estuaries and bays, a sailor truly appreciates coastal navigation.

Some people wish to take to the sea merely for the pleasure of seagoing itself. The word *yachting* fittingly describes that activity. Many people participate in this sport, from the child in a small sailboat to the solitary sailor who has won the most prestigious racing prize.

Yachting has experienced spectacular growth during the past fifty years, and the number of ports has increased. (The boat in this photograph is about to land on the ancient island of Corsica, off the coast of France.) Would-be sailors might learn the ropes from a relative or a friend. Or they can attend yachting school, several of which have grown up along the coasts in many parts of the world.

Not everyone can be a prizewinning sailor, but every person can begin a love story with the ocean. The sea provides pleasure, arouses awe, and in this sense provides a true schooling for life.

Oyster farming, an ecology-based trade

Oyster farmers take advantage of spring tides to tend to their beds at low tide. These toilers of the sea are surely the most ecologically minded workers of the maritime world.

The barge-like ships ply back and forth in the shallow water. Are these fishermen at work — or farmers? The truth is, they are both!

For centuries, oysters lived in layers near the seashore. That made it easy for early humans to find oysters to eat. Then, in the nineteenth century, demand for oysters increased and the natural beds began disappearing. But not so fast! People invented the idea of raising oysters in enclosures called beds. That's how oyster farming was born.

Along many coastal areas, oyster beds expanded. (This picture shows oyster farming taking place off the coast of France.) And despite diseases that sometimes kill them off, the oysters are still there in ever-greater numbers.

Oyster farmers are both sailors and farmers. They have a harsh job to do. From collecting baby oysters to raising and packing them, the farmers must carry out a variety of tasks before they can even sell their product. The whole process – from collecting to selling — takes three or four years, but the results help feed the world.

Workers of the salt marshes

In summer, at day's end, workers harvest the salt that the sun has turned to crystals.

Look down — and guess what you see. They look like checkerboards, mosaics, or patchworks when seen from the sky. They are really the salt marshes of the South of France. It's a stunning landscape created entirely by — and for — humans.

For centuries people have been farming salt from these areas. Salt is a valuable basic commodity that gives taste to food and allows it to be preserved, too.

First, people dig canals into the marshes. Seawater then flows into pools that become shallower and shallower. The water evaporates with the help of the sun and the wind. Finally, in the shallowest pools during the summer, when evaporation is at its peak, almost no water remains. Salt collecting can now begin.

Today, salt marshes have almost disappeared because of competition from the salt industry. But the workers of the few remaining salt marshes still continue their work, maneuvering through their salt marsh maze, accompanied by the birds, the sun, and the sea.

Keeper of the Kéréon Lighthouse

At the end of the day, before lighting the beacon, the lighthouse keeper checks to see that the automatic beacon in his lighthouse is in good working order.

Today most lighthouses work by themselves, but that hasn't always been true. In the past, the lighthouses had to have their attendants, people called lighthouse keepers. Their job was to light the "fire" in the lens, ensure that it worked well, and extinguish it at daybreak.

The fortunate keepers were those whose lighthouses were located on solid ground. Most of them lived with their families in small houses backed up against the tower.

But others performed their duties in lighthouses situated on the open ocean, far from any civilization, at the mercy of the sea. For entire weeks, they had only another keeper for company. During raging winter storms their stay at the lighthouse could be prolonged indefinitely, while waves often surged over the light and the tower itself shook on its foundations.

Today few lighthouses remain out at sea. The others are controlled automatically and operated from dry land. With the time of the lighthouse keepers passing away, a bit of the poetry of the open ocean is fading and vanishing, too.

A beacon in the night

At the furthest western point of the European continent, where the land ends, we find the lighthouse of Créac'h. At its feet lies a beautiful museum of lighthouse history and sea rescues.

They number in the thousands on all of the world's coasts. From Cape North to Cape Horn, from New York to Vladivostok, they light up each dangerous spit of land, each invisible sand bank, each isolated reef, each port entrance. They are the lighthouses, sending out their signals of hope and safety to weary and frightened sailors.

Some lighthouses are famous, such as Eddystone in Great Britain, which the sea twice destroyed. But perhaps the most famous lighthouse of all is the Alexandria Lighthouse, in Egypt, which ancient people thought of as one of the wonders of the world.

Each lighthouse has its own "language," its own way of blinking. The rhythms change, and the colors change, too. This photograph shows the Créac'h Lighthouse on the coast of France. It sends two white flashes forty-five miles out into the ocean every ten seconds.

The lighthouse towers are like sentinels of the sea. As they help ships locate dangerous coasts, they are witnesses to an old and precious history.

Storm warning

On days of heavy weather, the channel appears narrow, even for knowledgeable seamen.

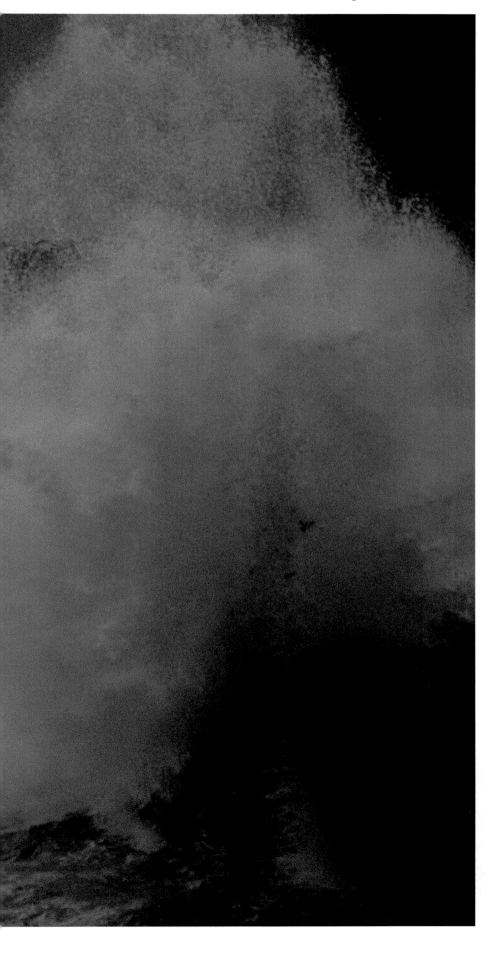

Danger! Get to shore at once! Take cover! Hurricane, tornado, typhoon, cyclone, or squall—storms take various forms and many names. Yet their effect is always much the same! Wind is the driving force—the more it blows, the wilder the sea; and, if wind starts to rage, so does the sea itself!

How exactly do we measure the ocean's many moods? A certain Sir Francis Beaufort invented a scale that bears his name and is used to describe the condition of the sea. Number one on the scale means that the waves are motionless: it's dead calm. Number three refers to a mild breeze that changes to a stiff, then heavy breeze. Starting at force seven on the scale, it's wise to lower your sails. Then, at eight, nine, and ten, the sea becomes increasingly fierce and the swell becomes heavier and heavier. At eleven and twelve, it's a hurricane—the sea seethes with foam, masts splinter, and the breakers are monstrous.

No seagoing person or any ship can claim to be stronger than the ocean. This photograph, taken off the French coast, says it all.

Shipwreck on the high sea

This shipwreck on the open sea resulted from poor reckoning.

"Hurry! Into the lifeboats. We're going down!" On the night of April 14, 1912, the *Titanic*, a new British-built ocean liner which, it was thought, could not sink, struck an iceberg in the North Atlantic and plunged to the bottom, dragging 1,500 passengers and crew with it to an icy death.

The wreck of the *Titanic* is probably the most famous shipwreck of all. But others are well known, too. The most recent was the Soviet nuclear submarine *Kursk*. Besides these, there have been countless unnamed ships that have sunk, from sailboats to freighters to fishing boats.

In our time, fortunately, shipwrecks have become a rarer occurrence and take fewer victims. Radios make it possible to call for help, weather forecasts are increasingly accurate, and helicopters can come to the rescue far from shore. (This photograph shows a ship, broken in two and sinking, near the coast of France.) Nevertheless, shipwrecks continue to happen. It's as though the sea wants to remind us that it's still stronger than we are.

Rescue at sea

A boat breaks down and begins to sink. A call goes out. Lucky for the caller and the crew, a rescue boat or a rescue helicopter arrives in the nick of time.

In many French ports that open onto the high seas, you can see green and orange patrol boats bearing the initials SNSM. These are rescue craft belonging to the National Sea Rescue Company. These strong boats hurry to the rescue of those who ask for their help, whether it's a yacht owner, a windsurfer, or someone fishing near the coast.

Despite the courage of these rescuers, they can be effective only near the coastline. Farther out on the open ocean, rescue is the province of high sea tugboats, extremely strong boats that can tow ships one hundred times bigger than they are. Helicopters, too, (as you can see in this picture) intervene to save property and lives.

To develop rescue plans fully, agencies set up their offices along the coasts. When the alarm sounds, these agencies alert the rescue services and coordinate their activity. The agencies play an essential role in preserving safety at sea. But no matter who they are, the people who perform ocean rescues must be clear-headed, strong, and brave.

Heavy weather and dead calm

By day and by night, and in rough weather or calm, fishermen ply their trade.

"We're heading out to sea today, but what will the weather be like?" It's an old question. "Wind from the east, 'tis no good for man or beast," goes an old sailor saying. Little by little, however, with the aid of increasingly precise instruments, a science called meteorology was born.

The invention of the barometer, which measures atmospheric pressure (that is, the weight of the air) was a tremendous leap forward. When the pressure is low, the air rises and cools, causing cloud formation. But when the pressure is high, air descends and heats up, chasing away the clouds.

Since the 1950s, numerous ships devoted to gathering meteorological information have been supplying data to the world's weather centers. This data includes atmospheric pressure, wind force, water temperature, and much more.

Today, satellites and computers are taking on the job of monitoring conditions. Because of these advances, ships now have ample warning of bad weather. True sailors will continue to rely on their instincts, while at the same time using information provided by technology.

weather satellite

Offshore platform on the open ocean

These offshore oil facilities are separated, yet a platform connects them—on one side is everything relating to oil extraction; on the other side is everything needed for oil reduction. This arrangement helps avoid the risk of fire.

In the beginning were the derricks, tall metal towers that made it possible to pump oil on land from the earth's depths. From Iraq to Texas, and from Borneo to Venezuela, people collected petroleum, or black gold, wherever it gushed out.

But the world's energy needs are continually increasing. So, what next? People decided to search for petroleum where it remained hidden — underneath the ocean floor. To do this, they created gigantic offshore drilling platforms (like the one seen in this photograph, off the coast of Scotland) erected in the open ocean. It's a true international gathering on these platforms—sailors, drilling teams, cooks, and others from many countries must live and work together, sometimes for many weeks at a time because of the distance from shore.

Of course, the work is harder on the high seas than it is on land. It was necessary to design facilities that could withstand storms in order to drill where the geologists' data suggested oil might be found. For better or worse, these gigantic constructions in the ocean have now become part of the marine seascape.

Framework of an old ship

A daunting adventure is in progress: the reconstruction of the frigate *Hermione*, on which, in 1780, French general Lafayette departed to join the American revolutionaries fighting for their independence.

You may think this photograph is some kind of optical illusion. It's not. It's actually the complex framework of an old-time ship. Look at the detail. Try to imagine the hard work!

All the early ships had one thing in common—they were made of wood. Iron and steel weren't used until the beginning of the nineteenth century, at first sparingly and then in ever-increasing quantities until wood was eliminated completely.

The "shipwright" was the person who knew how to use wood to build ships. He was known as the "master of the axe." It was a noble profession that disappeared as the years passed. Then something strange happened. As more people savored the joys of sailing, they also discovered the beauty of the old ships. Modern "shipwrights" went back to work. The tools of long ago gave way to modern machines, but the know-how was still there!

Today wooden boats are everywhere, either restored or built new. Once again, the masters of the axe are producing beautiful work.

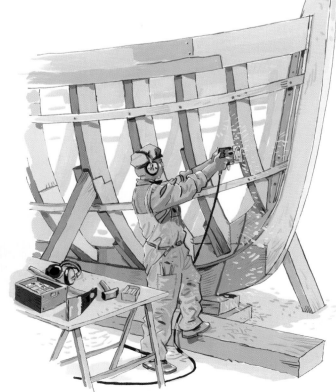

The merchant marine

A supertanker clears the oil terminal at Saint-Nazaire, France, after unloading its cargo of black gold.

Besides the navy and the many yacht owners, there is another seagoing arm as old as the world. This is the merchant marine. For thousands of years, the sea has served as a commercial route. The Phoenicians, the Arabs, the Chinese, and the Greeks, to mention only a few, used their ships to carry and exchange the most diverse commodities.

Today, ships intended for the transport of goods are called freighters. Their cargo is known as freight.

Modern freighters are becoming increasingly specialized. Wine tankers carry wine, grain ships transport wheat or corn, gas tankers hold gas, and oil tankers (like the one in this photograph) carry petroleum.

Workers put various goods into containers, each of which is a kind of huge rectangular box.

Of course, freighters travel more slowly than airplanes, but they can carry much more. You would need a fleet of planes to transport the wheat that is carried in ships each day. That's why the merchant marine is still crossing the oceans of the world.

The thrill of the regatta

The race is on. The wind is blowing at more than thirty knots. The crew of this racing yacht is tacking off Mission Bay, on the California coast.

Regattas are races in which sailboats compete against each other. The boats move forward along the same line and head for a buoy positioned on the open sea. After they reach the buoy and circle around it, they return as quickly as possible to the starting point. The first sailboat to cross the finish line wins. Many rules make sure that this test of speed and endurance runs as smoothly as possible.

There are regattas for all levels. And the size of the boat determines the length of the course.

The most prestigious of these races is still the America's Cup, first run in 1851.

Not just any boat can enter the major races. Cup contenders, you might say, are "dream boats." They are designed by the foremost architects and manned by the best crews. They also cost mind-boggling sums of money, which is why, at the beginning, the Cup was reserved for multimillionaires. But today sponsors give money to help people build competitive boats. And the progress of the race, which receives ever-increasing media coverage, now draws millions of television viewers every year.

An egret on its perch

From atop its perch alongside a river, this egret surveys its prey.

The oceans and rivers of the world aren't home only to the creatures that live in the water. Along the docks and coasts, and on the beaches and cliffs, seabirds belong to the marine seascape, too. Some of these birds do not venture far from shore; but others can travel hundreds of miles from land.

There are many species of seabirds. Most are especially well adapted to life on the sea. They often have webbed feet positioned far to the rear of their body, giving them greater stability when they float on the water. Some even have a gland in the corner of the eye that allows them to remove excess sea salt, which is harmful to them. The egret, shown in this photograph, has long legs for wading in shallow water, and a long thin beak well made for plucking its fish dinner from down below.

But the king of the oceans is certainly the albatross. When fully spread, its wingspan may exceed twelve feet. It comes to land only to reproduce. It can soar for hours at the center of the heaviest storms and—listen to this—sleeps in the hollows of the waves. Hail to the albatross!

puffin

herring gull

albatross

The fishermen's departure

Seaward, ho! People still use these traditional boats in many countries where they make their living by taking to the rough seas.

People have been fishing since the dawn of time. In many cultures of the past, whole populations lived only by fishing, and today, in certain parts of the world, they still do.

There are a thousand ways to fish, from the solitary Breton fisherman in his dinghy to the huge Russian and Japanese factory ships. But the principle is always the same—bring back to land the greatest number of fresh fish possible. To do this, the holds of modern trawlers allow those who fish to keep their cargo cold and, therefore, to stay out at sea for weeks.

But a new problem is emerging. In our time, many maritime areas are overfished, and some fish species are disappearing. Governments have enacted measures to limit areas where fishing is permitted, to set the maximum number of catches allowed, and to restrict the size of the fish that can be caught. In this way, fish populations in the oceans will remain constant, or even grow, and an important source of life and food will remain for future generations.

Bird stuck in an oil slick

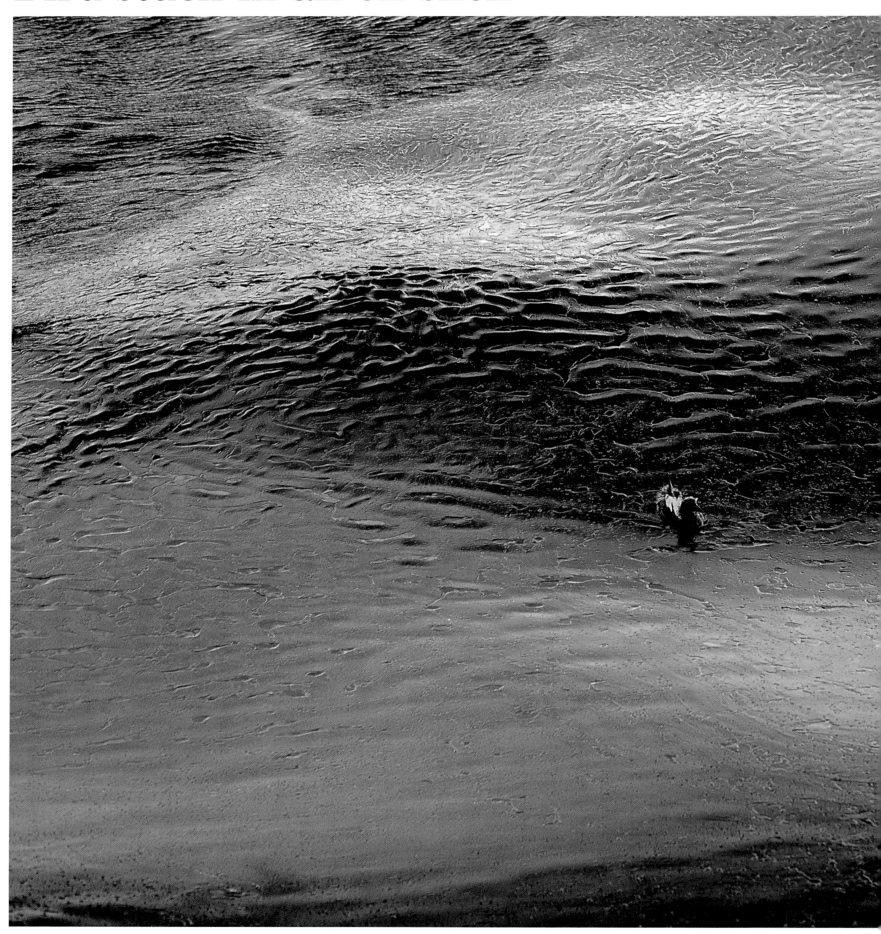

On December 20, 1999, the first oil slicks flowing out of the holds of the *Erika* approached Belle-Isle, France. This oil-bound gannet sends out a call for help, but the photographer high above in his helicopter remains a powerless spectator.

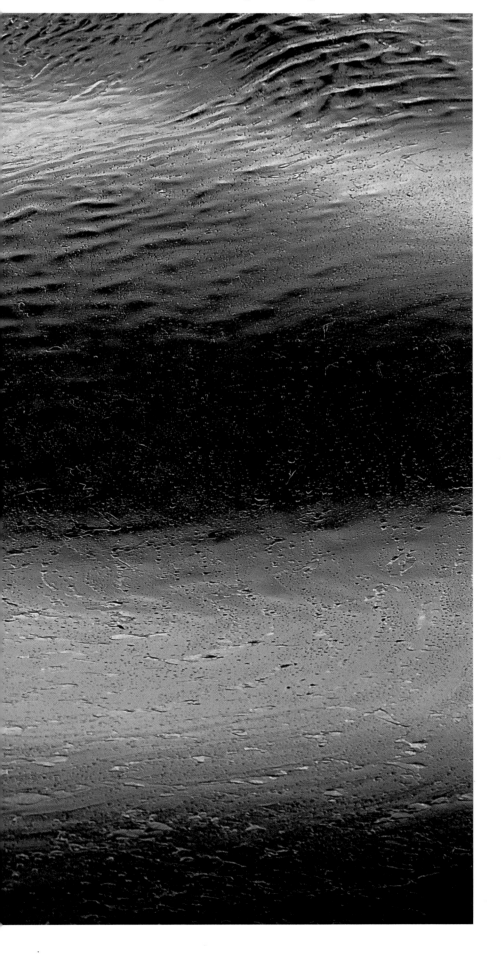

The oceans are so vast! Indeed, people were once led to believe the sea was immortal. But they were wrong, and we are just now beginning to realize this fact.

First, of course, there have been the spectacular disasters. Hundreds of thousands of tons of oil leaked from holds ripped open on the shipwrecked Amoco *Cadiz* and *Erika*. We all remember pictures of oil-stained beaches, suffocated fish, and seabirds transformed by the oil slick into dying statues.

But maritime pollution isn't limited to these huge catastrophes alone. Some oil tankers illegally clean out their tanks at sea; freighters silently dump barrels filled with nuclear waste into the ocean, and cities even discharge sewage into the sea.

The sea will not remain unchanged. Signs tell us of problems to come: vanishing fish stocks, toxic algae, and more. Let's hope humans remember the importance of the oceans—before it's too late!

Return of the *Belém*

In late October 1995, the *Belém* returns to the Atlantic after summering in the Mediterranean. Tall and forceful when riding the waves, it has regained the nobility of its one-time, long-distance runs.

The photograph gives you an idea of both the sea's power and the bravery of those who sailed in yesterday's great ships. But—believe it or not— some people still sail in such ships today!

Every year, in different ports on the globe, the great yachts gather from all over the world. From Colombia and Norway, Great Britain and the United States, the biggest yachts in the world, the giants of the sea, suddenly surge into view with sails flying. It is as if the past were to reappear in the present, in all its old majesty and beauty.

As in all shows, there are stars—boats that arouse everyone's admiration. Surely one such boat is the *Esmeralda*. Built in 1927, it belonged to the Spanish navy before becoming the training ship of the Chilean navy. A total of twenty-one officers and 140 sailors are onboard. France is represented by the *Belém*, a three-masted steel ship built in Nantes in 1896. Originally, it was used to carry cocoa beans. But today the *Belém*, operated by five officers and eleven crew members, is used to train those who wish to learn the traditional techniques of sailing ships.

Onboard maneuver

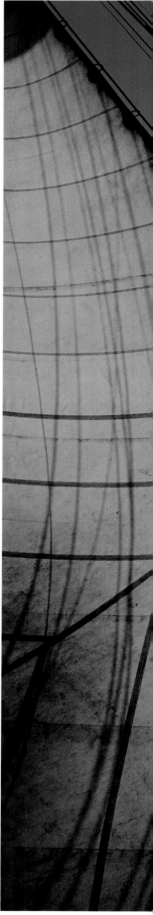

It may seem a simple thing to tie a knot, but those who take to the sea know it's not that simple at all!

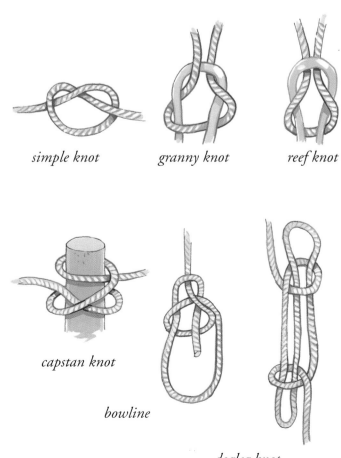

The art of tying knots is as old as sailing itself. A sailing ship has hundreds of ropes that raise and adjust the sails. Other ropes moor the ship to the dock. Beyond that, each rope has its own name. And beware to those who tie a knot badly!

There are, of course, many different kinds of knots. Some are quite simple, such as the reef knot, the granny knot, and the capstan knot. Others are complicated, such as the bowline, or extremely complicated, such as the dogleg knot. Each knot had a specific use on the great sailing ships.

Even today, the science of knots remains essential for those who sail yachts. One obvious reason for that is probably this: there's nothing more humiliating than watching your boat drift away because it was poorly tied down!

simple knot   *granny knot*   *reef knot*

capstan knot

bowline

dogleg knot

Child playing on the beach

This Polynesian boy, like children everywhere, loves to dig in the sand and splash in the water.

Ah, a day at the beach! Vast or tiny, made of fine sand or pebbles, beaches throughout the world attract millions of men, women, and children each year.

Beachgoing was made popular during the middle of the nineteenth century by a relative of Emperor Napoleon III. This cousin, a duke, started the fashion of swimming in the sea on France's Normandy coast. Since that time, thousands of oceanside resorts have flourished all over the globe.

Beaches encourage all forms of recreation, from getting a tan to building sand castles to playing volleyball. Even more, there are the pleasures of the sea itself. Here one can wade, windsurf, sail, and, above all else, swim.

During the past 150 years, water recreation and the seaside tourist trade have become more and more popular. But there's a reverse side to this coin: there is the excessive concrete sprawl along the coasts to accommodate summer residents; there is the increased pollution; and the list goes on. The problem humans face is how to enjoy the beaches and seas of the world— but keep them clean and usable at the same time.

Ships stranded in sand at a port

Little by little, the sea recedes from the Port of Nouadhibou, leaving an old fishing fleet sunk in the sand.

The ocean is always on the move, rising slightly or falling back. And when it does, the shorelines change, too. You don't have to study prehistory to realize this fact.

During the Middle Ages, for example, the French king Saint Louis departed for the crusades from a French town called Aigues-Mortes. But today this town is located several miles from shore. Why? Because the ocean has withdrawn over time. Another example is the Aral Sea between Kazakhstan and Uzbekistan. Shallow but full of fish, it once supported an entire population of fishermen, but enormous irrigation projects that were completed under the Soviet regime have dried it up, slowly but steadily. Today you can see trawlers that have run aground miles from the water.

In a similar fashion, on the coast of Mauritania (check out the photograph), advancing sands have captured a number of trawlers in their clutches.

Yes, truly, the oceans and their various shorelines are always changing.

One strange boat

The hydrofoil skims over the water on its initial trials. One man dreamed about it; another man built it.

It is one of humanity's dreams: to build a sailboat which, because of its speed and nimbleness, can lift off the water and soar like an albatross. Sometimes dreams can become a reality.

Eric Tabarly was passionate about traditional boats; at the same time, he studied every new technical innovation relating to the sea. He was the one who, beginning in 1976, experimented with a strange craft designed by an engineer, Alain de Bergh.

In 1979, a boat piloted by Tabarly and a friend took second place in the two-person Lorient-to-Bermuda Transatlantic Race. The boat traveled fast, very fast, but was too heavy to truly take off. Even stronger, lighter materials were needed.

Then in the late 1990s, the hydrofoil was put in the water. Alain Thébaut was the designer and skipper. The boat reached top speeds of thirty-nine knots, but later runs would soon measure forty-five knots (that is, around fifty-five miles per hour), an absolutely stunning record on water.

Where will the hydrofoil go from here? Faster and faster? Into the air at last? Who can say?

Low tide and high tide

The two photographs show the low and high tides at a coastal region of France. The difference in water level, as you can see, is astonishing.

What causes the tides? The answer to this has to do with things far from Earth. The sun and the moon exert strong forces on our Earth and on the oceans that cover it. When the moon is positioned just above the sea, it pulls the water toward it, and the water rises. As the moon continues its path in the sky, the water, no longer pulled upward, falls back again.

But there are no tides in the Mediterranean Sea. Why? It's an enclosed body of water in which water can neither rush in nor recede. Elsewhere, the sea rises and falls at different paces, depending on the place and season, the water depth, winds, and atmospheric pressure. In Tahiti, for example, a slight tide occurs at noon. But in the Bay of Fundy, on the eastern coasts of Canada and the U.S., the difference between high and low tide is nearly sixty feet.

Every six hours, the tides give a rhythm to life along most seacoasts. When the ocean is low, it sometimes recedes very far, leaving boats aground. Then it rises again. Ships float and waves return once more to lap against the cliffs.

Underwater diving

For thirty years, Albert Falco assisted Captain Jacques Cousteau, the famous underwater explorer. Today, for the pleasure of it, Falco continues to film the fauna that still amazes him.

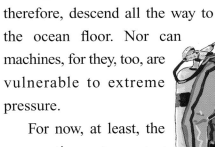

It's yet another of humanity's oldest dreams: to venture deep into the undersea world where, according to legend, cities have been swallowed up and mysterious, never-seen creatures reside.

But humans can't breathe underwater. To do so, they have invented machines, from the simple oxygen bottle to the most sophisticated submarine, which allow them to descend to the greatest ocean depths. There divers can locate sunken wrecks, repair oil-drilling rigs and, quite simply, admire the ocean depths as they drift alongside coral atolls.

For the time being, though, humans have only opened the door to the undersea world a crack. As soon as the diver reaches a certain depth, the water pressure on the lungs becomes increasingly strong, and it is necessary to make a very slow ascent. Failure to obey this rule can cause accidents that often prove fatal. Humans cannot, therefore, descend all the way to the ocean floor. Nor can machines, for they, too, are vulnerable to extreme pressure.

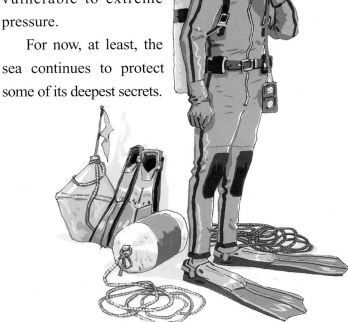

For now, at least, the sea continues to protect some of its deepest secrets.

Eric Tabarly, an extraordinary seaman

Seen through a tangle of ropes and knots, Eric Tabarly guides the *Pen Duick* through calm waters.

The extraordinary seaman Eric Tabarly is probably the best known of all French sailors. After studying at the French Naval Academy, the school that trains future officers for France's fleet, Tabarly was assigned to different naval duties. Later he devoted himself entirely to his great passion, sailing.

Eric started by buying from his father the wreck of the family boat, the *Pen Duick*, a small sailboat that had been built in Ireland in 1898. Soon, the name would become familiar to many. It would be followed by *Pen Duick 1, 2, 3, 4,* and *5*—all sailboats, all different from each other. On these boats, Eric won most of the world's major seagoing races, starting with the English Transatlantic Race of 1964.

Eric loved classic sailboats and old sailing ships, but he continued to study new technologies. Of all his boats, however, his favorite would remain *Pen Duick 1*. Indeed, he was onboard this craft when tragedy occurred one night in June 1998. It was on this night that Eric Tabarly disappeared off the coast of Wales, leaving behind the memory of a great sailor and a man who truly loved the sea.

The magic of the sea

1. In the distance on the left, the small Clare Island Lighthouse in Ireland. 2. The Cordouan Lighthouse at the mouth of the Gironde River in France.
3. Beaulieu River, England. 4. Light breeze and surf.